DESIGN HACKING

Resourceful Innovation and
Sustainable Self-Reliance

By Scott Burnham

Print Edition December 2019

Original Essay Copyright 2010 Scott Burnham

ISBN-13: 978-1-945971-03-7

Written by Scott Burnham

For all permissions and correspondence, contact Scott Burnham: sb@scottburnham.com

"Adopt a hacker attitude towards all forms of knowledge: not only to learn UNIX or Windows NT to hack this or that computer system, but to learn economics, sociology, physics, biology to hack reality itself. It is precisely the "can do" mentality of the hacker, naive as it may sometimes be, that we need to nurture everywhere."[i]

- *Manuel Deland*

Hackers Build Things

In 1971 Californian John Draper received a phone call from a friend, informing him of a fascinating discovery. A toy whistle packaged in boxes of Captain Crunch cereal could, when blown, emit a perfect 2600 hertz pitch. The relevance of this was lost on Draper until his friend explained that this was the exact frequency required to trick the phone exchange into thinking that the phone emitting this tone was an operator, thus enabling the person to make calls anywhere in the world free of charge. All you needed to do was dial a certain number and blow the whistle into the mouthpiece of the phone, and seconds later communicating with the rest of the world for free was literally at your fingertips. The world's phone networks had just been hacked.

Several months after learning of the telephone frequency hack, Draper went on to build 'blue boxes', small devices that mimicked multiple phone frequencies to expand the reach and functionality of the phone system hack. At the height of his infamous 'phone phreaking' streak, as it was known, Esquire magazine ran an article featuring his exploits[ii].

A university student named Steve Wozniak read the article, and contacted Draper, convincing him to come to Wozniak's dorm room to teach him and a friend more about blue boxes. Draper tutored them on the techniques to create the devices and alter existing technologies to hack the phone system. Wozniak credits this phase as being instrumental in his career of technology innovation, as did his friend who joined him in the tutoring sessions, Steve Jobs. Fuelled and funded by creating and selling the phone hacking blue boxes, Wozniak and Jobs started a small company called Apple Computers and set up shop in a garage to start work on their next 'box' - one that would have far more impact on the world - the personal computer.

If you trace the iPhone, the iPod, the Mac and the first personal computer back to their source, you'll find a hacker.

In any exploration of hacking, there is first a need to clarify the term. The word 'hacker' has a certain infamy in contemporary culture, bearing responsibility for security breaches and online intrusions. As Eric Raymond writes in his text How to Become a Hacker, clarification is important. The practitioners representing the darker side of the term, says Raymond, "loudly call themselves hackers, but aren't … real hackers call these people 'crackers' and want nothing to do with them … being able to break security doesn't make you a hacker any more than hotwiring cars makes you an automotive engineer." In short: "hackers build things, crackers break them."[iii]

But hacking is really just today's name for the personal creative spirit that has always underpinned human ingenuity. The farmer reworking a piece of machinery to perform a different function than it was originally designed for, or the housewife cutting the bottom of a plastic bottle to make it into a scoop: hacking is our response when the resources at hand come up short.

It is only recently that the word has emerged as a collective term for a personal response to, and triumph over, the limitations of our physical world. The term itself was coined by the hobbyists who brought computers out of their academic origins and in the process determined that the existing tools and systems weren't sufficient for their needs, so set about to make the systems more interesting and useful.

Hacking and technological innovation have a long and mutually beneficial cat-and-mouse history. The first software companies gave computer users the freedom to install various components and to customise the settings; but if you wanted to go deeper into the system to alter the basic functions and foundation of the software or the system, you hit a wall. Some went about finding access points that would allow entry to the core of the system and enable alternative functions to be programmed in. Others set about to build 'open source' systems to allow full transparency and access to the system. The Linux operative system, the Apache web server (which runs the majority of the world's websites), the Firefox browser and numerous other applications are the results of the open source movement, born of the hacker's desire for access and permission.

As the open source movement wove innovation and openness into the fabric of the internet, the rapid growth of home computing and personal software made it possible to manipulate existing songs, videos, images and even 3D design schematics with ease. When the tools which were once the exclusive domain of professionals were put in the hands of millions of individual users and consumers, every tweak of a song

5

or manipulation of a photograph planted the ability to alter the aesthetics of the world a bit deeper.

While desktop applications and Web 2.0 services were giving us unparalleled means to modify and differentiate our digital world, our physical or analogue world of products and services was reaching a saturation point of sameness, as retail chains, big box stores and globalised brands proliferated.

Companies and retailers responded by making it easier for consumers to customise their products at the point of purchase, but within set limitations. Henry Ford joked that people can have any colour car they like, as long as it is black. The joke has lasted well, as retailers continue to boast of the customers' ability to tailor products to their needs - as long as their desires are among a specific set of options.

It is within this climate that hacking has evolved from the software to the hardware of our lives. Make magazine, a leading proponent of DIY technology and hacking methodologies gives the consumer a simple test to gauge the actual degree to which they are in control: "If you can't open it, you don't own it."[iv]

If retail and manufacturing's response to commercial sameness is to offer a limited range of customisation choices, then hacking is the individual's response: circumventing those limitations and creating new options on one's own terms. When this hacking ethos is applied to our relationship with design, it has a more fundamental charge - a return to design as a direct response to real problems faced by real people.

In 1969 Victor Papanek argued that the professionalisation of design had separated it from the "real world" [v]. Design cannot be separated from everyday life, he wrote, and by elevating its trained practitioners as professionals from those who are not so trained (amateurs), design begins to reference only itself, and fails to address real problems faced by real people. In this process of professionalisation, trial-and-error creativity has been lost. Hacking puts it back into the equation.

Hacking is about overcoming the limitations of an existing object, service or system which was set for one purpose, and finding an access point, intellectually or physically, where its original function can be expanded, altered, or improved to serve a new purpose or solve a problem. Hacking is not about aesthetics as much as purpose - the ultimate union of form and function.

"Hackers do what they do...", says researcher Julian Bleecker of the Near Future Laboratory, "not necessarily because they are designing something in the sense of disciplined design. They are making a thing - and often that thing doesn't look finished, which is almost part of the hacking sensibility... Bringing hacking to design can be unstable, but what hacking practices can teach are important - rapid construction, an appreciation and understanding of things that go below the surface features and bringing functionality into the design process.[vi]"

Increased activity surrounding design and hacking has spawned a small industry of websites and publications engaging with this growing trend.

Readymade magazine illustrates the craft and ingenuity of the individual as he or she goes about various home improvements using re-used and repurposed material; while Instructables.org has become the de-facto repository for instructions, videos and advice on how to hack almost anything one encounters in daily life. Make magazine has taken the hacker's creed as a call to action. Its manifesto, "The Maker's Bill of Rights", calls on manufacturers to follow such hackable principles as "if it snaps shut, it shall snap open", and "screws are better than glues".

One of the most iconic projects to emerge from hacking's infusion into the world of design is the global IKEA Hacker initiative. IKEA Hacker is an unofficial network of design hackers who share a passion for reworking IKEA products on their own terms and creating designs IKEA never planned. Assembling the flat-packed furniture of one of the world's most ubiquitous contemporary design brands and interpreting the language-neutral instructions are a rite of passage of any new apartment dweller or university student. But what if, comes the voice of the IKEA Hacker project, you assembled the furniture in a different way than IKEA tells you?

This simple question has birthed thousands of new creations from IKEA's set range of products. A Fjus bookshelf is assembled 'alternatively' from the instructions to make a pet's feeding and watering station. Kitchen units are re-assembled to become garage workshop stations. Salad tongs are fastened together to become light fixtures, and desks become children's playpens. Often the hackers will take the time to document the steps needed to imitate their hacks and make them available online, enabling an entire alternative product line to run parallel to the one in the catalogue.

IKEA Hacker has become something of a universal illustration of the interplay between hacking and design - ignore the issued instructions and devise your own. As well as the personal pleasure of making a unique or idiosyncratic product, there is an intellectual challenge in thoroughly understanding the intended rules of the designed object, then creating your own version according to your own rules. Phone hacker Draper shared this motivation. Though vilified by the media as the man who almost brought down America's phone system in the 1970s, that was never the intention of his hacks. For him, "it was about taking the system apart, to make the thing better. To make it do better things. Cooler things."[vii]

Of course, both the pleasure derived from subverting IKEA's instructions and the desire for a system to do 'cooler things' come from a fairly privileged perspective. For most of the world, things which function in 'cooler' ways is a dream several steps beyond immediate necessity. In developing nations in particular, function and necessity are the driving principles, usually corresponding to a limited pool of resources and materials to work with.

Learning from Repair Culture

The mobile phone has become the Swiss Army knife of the developing world, an essential tool for conducting almost any form of business. Yet in emerging markets and nations, the stock supply of phones is of a much lower functionality than the users require. In response, a parallel industry of informal local 'repair' shops has emerged to hack upgraded functions and services into the available phones. The definition of repair is extended from fixing something that is broken, to repairing its limitations.

Nokia's Jan Chipchase has spent years researching mobile phone use in cities throughout China, Africa, and India looking at the ways in which people there use and modify their mobile phones beyond their original specification. Far outside the reach of official service centres and sales offices, Chipchase encounters mobile phone markets that "stretch across numbers of streets and shopping arcades and includes hundreds of small shops and stalls".

"What sets these locations apart from cities in more 'emerged' markets? Aside from the scale of what's on sale there is a thriving market for device repair services ranging from swapping out components to re-soldering circuit boards to reflashing phones in a language of your choice. Repairs are often carried out with little more than a screwdriver, a toothbrush (for cleaning contact points) the right knowledge and a flat surface to work on. Repair manuals (which appear to be reverse engineered) are available, written in Hindi, English and Chinese and can even be subscribed to, but there is little evidence of them being actively used. Instead many of the repairers rely on informal social networks to share knowledge on common faults, and repair techniques. It's often easier to peer over the shoulder of a neighbour than open the manual itself… The informal repair services that are offered are quite simply driven by necessity."[viii]

With necessity as the driver, the repair culture has morphed into a culture of 'street hacks', repairing not what is broken, but what the phone lacks. Ancient phones that would have been discarded years ago by most in the West leave the repair shops with dual SIM card slots soldered in to switch networks at will, or a reworked handset with new keys for increased functionality or language accommodation.

Rather than going after the street hackers with lawyers or sending in the police with bin bags, Nokia's response to the street hacks and repair cultures has been exceptional: learn from them. Chipchase's years of research in some of the most remote cities, slums and favelas bears witness to this strategy. Of greater testimony is the fact that Nokia developed a concept phone in 2008, the 'Remade', using recycled materials and based on the research and inspiration gained from street-level innovation and developing world users.

"What can we learn from informal repair cultures?" asks Chipchase. "Given the benefit to 'bottom of the pyramid' consumers are there elements of the repair ecosystem that can be exported to other cultures? Can the same skills be applied to other parts of the value chain? Given the range of resources and skills available what would it take to turn cultures of repair into cultures of innovation?"

In a recent TED Talk, Chipchase summed up his research on street repair and hack culture in a message to the design world: "if you're smart, you'll be observing street innovation and applying this to inform and infuse what and how you design."[ix]

Of equal utilitarian value to the mobile phone in developing regions is the bicycle. A fundamental tool for transportation, commerce, industry, and even energy production, the bicycle has its own equally diverse history of hacks and modifications. Decades of hacking and modifications to the bicycle are embedded in that staple of Western leisure and sporting culture, the mountain bike.

In the 1960's and 70's, weekend cyclists began venturing off the paved roadways on the thin frames and tires of their road bikes, quickly finding they were of little use and short lifespan off-road. Slowly and steadily over the years, in garages and backyards, bicycle frames were reconfigured and re-welded, supports added, tires enlarged, and handlebars reshaped, until in the 1980's the current hearty but commercial mountain bike emerged.

The difference emerges again between the 'leisure' hacks of the developed West, and the more direct improvisations of the developing world. Street vendors in India, for example, have tweaked and altered the bicycle into a seemingly infinite number of variations that have little to do with sport, allowing them to turn a standard bicycle into a multi-functional commercial unit. Helium tanks are welded to the backs of a bicycle carrying balloons and party favours, grills are attached to mobile food vendor bikes, racks, shelves and platforms are welded onto structures of leather goods dealers, pot vendors - the list is long and growing.

As with Nokia's embrace of the street phone-hacking sector, the street hacks on Indian bicycles are stimulating design projects in the developed world. In 2008, New Delhi designer Gunjan Gupta launched the 'cyclerecyclecycle' design project as part of Urban Play in Amsterdam at the Experimenta design biennale. Gupta installed a version of an Indian bicycle repair shop on the street in Amsterdam, inviting the bicycle-obsessed Dutch to modify their own bikes in the manner of India's utilitarian street vendors.

Africa also has a long history of using modified bicycles for trade and commerce with a range of ingenuity on par with India. A new breed of African hackers and innovators are digging even more deeply into the functionality of the bicycle, gaining inspiration from its rudimentary mechanics for a range of uses beyond the simple transportation function. In Kenya a mobile phone charging station powered by the rotation of the tires as it travels from village to village was launched this year[x]; In Tanzania, Bernard Kiwia created a "pedal powered hacksaw for the disabled", a water pump for his village and a drill press by using the pedal mechanisms of bicycles[xi].

For William Kamkwamba, a 14-year-old farmer in Malawi, the bicycle served as an inspiring baseline design for a project to benefit his entire village. During a drought in 2001, Kamkwamba's family hit hard times, and he spent his idle time in the local library, where he came across a book on windmills and wind energy. With nothing but the pictures in the book to guide him, he then visited a local scrap yard to source materials that would roughly serve the function of the windmill's parts - a tractor fan, shock absorber, PVC piping, and other components.

Kamkwamba set about assembling the parts with the pictures of advanced wind turbines as a guide, and at the centre of the home-made wind generator was a bicycle, providing the frame of the machine and an efficient power transfer mechanism - the pedals, chain, and rear wheel of the bike.

Hacking methodologies have been particularly useful in developing nations for increasing the functionality of mobile phones and deploying the bicycle to serve other needs. They are equally useful in addressing one of the mightiest and most impenetrable systems in Western culture as well - the interlinked system of municipal regulations and town planning processes.

In many ways, the city itself is emblematic of the tension between dictated use and the resourcefulness of the hacker. The physical landscape of the city is deliberately designed to be a solid, non-malleable terrain of order and structure. Buildings, pavements, bridges and walls shape our movement and define our limitations. But as with any structured system, its limitations can become catalysts for creativity. Enter skateboarders, freewheel bikers, parkour/freerunners, urban climbers and explorers. These are the frontline of urban hackers, viewing the city as a literal playground. Stair railings are now ramps. Walls are balancing beams. Rooftops are launching platforms. This brand of hacker creates an infinite amount of space from the finite confines of the city. They create new paths of travel, inventing new possibilities and layering new dimensions on the established structure of the city. The extension of a hacking mentality at work in the modern urban landscape is endless – graffiti artists using the surfaces of the city as a canvas and message board, street vendors viewing the heavily trafficked and tourist areas of the city as makeshift commercial zones.

Hacking has now gone beyond these terrain trespasses to begin addressing the shortcomings of the city's systems and processes. There are obvious reasons for the rules and regulations at work in the city, but often they focus more on prohibition than permission; on what you can't rather than what you can do in and to shared spaces and services. To invoke Henry Ford again, citizens can engage with public services any way they like - within the set list of rules.

Creating Opportunity with Civic Hacks

A number of individuals and organisations have taken it upon themselves to engage in what could be called civic hacks: playing within the framework of the city's systems but altering them at the user level to perform different functions.

In the centre of Seville, Spanish architect Santiago Cirugeda wanted to build a playground for the neighborhood children. in 1997 he applied for permission and was denied. He then applied for permission to install a skip in front of his house on the pretext of clearing some construction debris. The skip was approved. He then set about installing a see-saw inside the skip for the children to play on.[xii]

In San Francisco, the Rebar collective is a group of four friends frustrated by the lack of green space in the city. They had petitioned the mayor's office with their concerns yet received no response. So, one afternoon in November 2005 they gathered some turf, a bench and some trees, pooled together several handfuls of quarters, and hacked the city's parking system to create a temporary park in a public parking space.

"Feeding the meter of a parking space enables one to rent precious downtown real estate, typically on a 1/2 hour to 2-hour basis. What is the range of possible occupancy activities for this short-term lease? PARK(ing) is an investigation into reprogramming a typical unit of private vehicular space by leasing a metered parking spot for public recreational activity.

We identified a site in an area of downtown San Francisco that is underserved by public outdoor space and is in an ideal, sunny location between the hours of noon and 2 p.m. There we installed a small, temporary public park that provided nature, seating, and shade.

Our goal was to transform a parking spot into a PARK(ing) space, thereby temporarily expanding the public realm and improving the quality of urban human habitat, at least until the meter ran out. By our calculations, we provided an additional 24,000 square-foot-minutes of public open space that Wednesday afternoon."[xiii]

Their PARK(ing) project is commemorated annually by enthusiasts worldwide. On 18 September each year an informal network of public space hackers hit the streets of their cities armed with the ingredients for a DIY public park and plenty of change for the parking meters.

Rebar are also notable for their work re-purposing San Francisco's curious breed of 'POPOS' - Privately Owned Public Spaces. These spaces - courtyards, plazas, rooftop gardens, and corporate atriums - are deemed to be public areas at the planning stage of the property's development but are usually so deeply hidden within corporate offices or otherwise private buildings that they deter public use.

Rebar researched "the explicit and unspoken rules" of these spaces within the city ordinances and bylaws and proceeded to program and advertise a series of public community activities in the private-public spaces, ranging from meditation classes to mid-day napping lounges. When challenged by security guards they had proof that what they were doing was entirely permissible. Later, the city of San Francisco enlisted Rebar to create an official map of all the spaces to promote their public use.

Further up the West coast of the United States, City Repair in Portland, Oregon wanted to turn the intersection of a residential neighborhood into a place for people, not just cars. When it seemed doubtful they could get permission from the city, they got a permit for a block party and built tea stands, book trade stations, and community information points all around the intersection. The spirit spread quickly, and people began giving over pieces of their private property to host some of the elements of the larger party. Once the block party ended, the partying crowds left revealed a series of temporary facilities for services the area had been asking for.

The city of Portland instinctively declared the structures illegal, until it was pointed out that through these hacks the city had actually progressed towards its own "livability goals" without spending any public funds. The city acquiesced. In time it granted an ordinance for the structures to remain, and later to be improved; and for similar structures to be formally built in other areas of the city. The residents' urban planning hack resulted in the improvement of over a dozen neighborhoods in the city using the "block party" template.

Urban hacks - from brazen temporary space-grabbing to guerilla performances of music and drama and art installations - inspire a new breed of civic engagement and take the sense of hacking far from its electronic origins.

In its essence, hacking exploits the tensions and barriers between objects, systems and people. What might happen when those tensions are addressed directly, and the barriers deliberately opened?

Adopting a Lego Attitude

At an industry level, it is difficult to find a company that has been more triumphant in both bottom-line benefits and brand success by opening up its product than Lego. This might seem an obvious philosophy for a company whose product is literally the building blocks for other people's creativity, but the company's own history of 'hackability' is complex.

When Lego began to expand its product line into pre-designed kits for specific objects, they instantly found that the kits were being combined with others, augmented, altered and re-designed; and instructions on how to do so being shared among enthusiast groups. It found itself with a vastly expanding and passionate user base that was taking Lego design into its own hands and has since defined the company's outlook. Shortly after it released a stand-alone application to allow customers to create Lego kits specific to their own designs, the application itself was hacked by its users.

"When Lego executives recently discovered that adult fans of the iconic plastic bricks had hacked one of the company's new development tools for digital designers, they did a surprising thing: They cheered.

Unlike executives at so many corporations, who would be loath to let their customers anywhere near the inner workings of their software tools, the Lego honchos saw an opportunity to lean on the collective thinking of an Internet community to improve their own product while bolstering relations with committed customers.

All it took was being open-minded enough to see that their biggest fans weren't trying to rip them off; they were trying to improve Lego's products in a way that, just maybe, the company's own designers hadn't thought of."[xiv]

Owing largely to the embrace of an open design mentality, Lego hacks have become creative legend. Outside the plethora of miniature movie scenes and mechanisms in homes around the world, the Dutch artist Jan Vormann uses the bricks to repair broken bits of buildings, and BBC Top Gear presenter James May created an entire life-size house using millions of the bricks, complete with bed and functioning bathroom.

The potential of adopting a Lego-style attitude is not lost on other manufacturers who have seen their own products being manipulated in unexpected ways. "We know about it," said an IKEA Executive when asked about IKEA Hacker, "but we also realise that we're having our own 'Lego moment', so we're just watching and enjoying".

As companies allow their customers to have a more direct involvement in the end design of their products, there is an opportunity to re-image manufacturing itself along hacking principles. To harness the potential of an open design mentality, designers and manufacturers should aim beyond simply being observers of the hacking to stimulating it as a move towards a new model for design and production.

There is a powerful economic and social argument to be made for opening the design and manufacturing process to hacking methodologies. Whether a symptom of a growing subculture or of resourcefulness in the face of a global recession, 'Hacklabs' are appearing in increasing numbers in Europe and the United States. Dedicated to "exchanging knowledge, designing worlds, experimenting with gizmos and devices"[xv], Hacklabs are publicly-run workshops that provide space, tools and tutoring for people to repurpose and re-appropriate things from their daily lives. Participants are flocking to Brooklyn's NYC Resistor Lab, London's Media Hacklab and Milan's LOA Hacklab to learn how to take things apart, how they work, and how to put them back together again, differently and to serve another purpose.

Hacklabs and the proliferation of online instructions for modifying and repurposing existing objects could be interpreted as another indicator that consumerism and globalism have left us jaded with commercial design. 'Closed' products imply that the consumers' needs have been decided by the professionals: we are being told what the products we buy are for rather being able to make them what we want them to be. In rebuttal, hacking is coming into mainstream parlance as a way to repurpose existing designs and objects in ways more precisely tailored to the user's needs and desires.

What if the design and manufacturing industry responded to this and implemented hacking as part of the manufacturing process of a product?

For the maker and manufacturer, the notion of releasing a product which allows itself to be altered and repurposed by the consumer turns one product into the potential of multiple products in the eyes of the end user.

Let us imagine going one step back from the release of the finished product and distributing the product at the design stage to small manufacturing facilities around the world, to local requirements and using local materials and labour.

Distributed production has been a longtime strategy for many companies in order to reduce shipping and other costs. By also employing distributed design and encouraging localised hacks of the source product, the local makers and manufacturers become the middle practitioners in the life of the product. Locally available materials reduce the carbon footprint of the final product. At the same time a local relationship is formed for future repairs or service. The design may be adjusted for local needs, and/or climate and cultural variations which are not possible to address at a universal design global scale.

This process of 'hackufacturing' is a necessary evolution in the face of globalised commerce and design. The intellectual property of the source design remains with the designer, while the alteration and realisation of the final product anchors it in the resources and realities of the local manufacturer.

The street-level mobile phone repair shops do this exceedingly well in Asia and Africa, where globally produced phones are hacked to address local needs in ways that could never be addressed at the global level. As Nokia does, the rest of the world's makers and manufacturers should look at these hubs of hacker activity not as illegal outposts, but as R&D labs for new methods of design and production.

Whether provoked by basic necessity or advanced consumer desire, hacking is a response to design falling short, withthe hacker stepping in to redress the gap between designer and the real world.

Almost 40 years on since he predicted it, there is little evidence that Papanek's warning about professional design distancing itself from the real world has not become true. An increasingly self-referential scene and a global industry of design festivals and conferences moves largely the same audience from one to the next. "Design Art" has moved the discipline further into galleries and away from problem-solving. The distance is growing between design and our needs, as is the ability for the proverbial man on the street to engage in a dialogue about design and his daily life.

This is not the case when you ask someone about their relationship with music, film, books, television, or even the attractiveness of their local park. Design is perceived as elevated from the daily realities and environments of most people, although its effects are more integral than almost any other creative discipline.

The way we interact with design differs significantly from how our consumption and relationship with other creative disciplines has evolved. The radio is awash with remixes and covers of classic songs; television and cinema offer endless adaptations and interpretations of literary works; and YouTube presents a seemingly endless stream of video remixes, mashups and alternative edits to enrich with the remix culture of the internet. The barrier between the medium and the individual has been broken down. When someone hears the remix of a song on the radio, it warms their relationship to the medium itself. It now seems more malleable in people's minds – more approachable, more open. By comparison, design as a discipline remains largely unyielding and closed.

The Benefits of Hacking

The emergence of a hacking culture which is now responding to the physical rather than the digital is evidence of a public will to repurpose the objects they own and of a desire for a new relationship with the objects and systems they buy and use. Hacking represents reciprocity between the user and the designer. While it complicates authorship and challenges the designer's usual instinct for control, hacking also breaks down barriers between design and people and yields significant benefits in the process.

Hacking creates new engagements between the product and the consumer.

The dominant model for design has placed the designer/maker at one end of the spectrum, and the consumer at the other. Hacking serves as a 'middle process' between creation and consumption, creating an opening for new design processes which are not about the use of new resources, but about the ingenuity to expand the potential of existing ones.

Hacking mandates relevance and necessity in design.

Hacking represents a return to a direct call and response between need and solution. There is nothing superfluous in a hacked product or system.

Hacking is resourceful.

Hackers are driven by a curiosity to find ways to augment and object or system for improvement, or to find new functions through tweaks and adjustments. By deepening their understanding and creating a number of possible applications, hackers represent a new approach to problem solving which increases the range of designed responses to society's needs.

Hacking creates abundance from limited resources.

To hack an object or a system is to take it from its original state and augment, improve, or re-work it to serve an alternative purpose. By expanding its function and form from its original singular state to one which might serve multiple other purposes, hackers create numerous design responses from one base.

Hacking finds the truth in systems.

The first thing software hackers do when they gain access to a program's source code is explore and share hidden code and functions not documented by the original programmers. When design hackers open and take apart products to rework them, the type and quality of wood found beneath the paint or the interior parts used are discussed widely. Hacking brings the inner realities of products to the surface. It reveals the complete aesthetic and exposes secrets.

Ultimately, hacking gives people a voice. Hacking creates new realities, options and possibilities from those we are given, whether commercial, social or civic. It offers forth the notion of a democratisation of design, by enabling the end user to be part of the process and not only on the receiving end of it.

Whether the model is re-working designs in IKEA Hacker or expanding the green space in the city through Park(ing), there is a triumphant message of individual resourcefulness and direct engagement when a hacker sensibility is applied to situations.

Most of all, hacking is evidence of our fundamental self-reliance in spite of professionalism, bureaucracy and industrial supply. In many ways, it is a return to, or a rediscovery of, the skills which saw us through our pre-consumerist times, when 'making do' with what you had to hand required inventiveness.

To relegate such activity to the realms of 'amateurism' is a dangerous dismissal, for it not only further deepens the 'us and them' disconnect between design and society but ignores the vast potential of the creative energies at work outside established channels.

Hacking presents significant challenge to the power structures embedded in form and use. Yet as desktop fabricators lower in price each year and more designers' works are being machined from CAD source files, it is obvious that the physical realisation of design will be increasingly dispersed and localised – why not allow the design process to become dispersed and localized with it?

The boom box remixes, loops, hacks and samples which first appeared on the steps of brownstone buildings in the Bronx decades ago were dismissed as marginal noise created by cultural outsiders. Today we recognise these same 'marginal' players as the forefathers of hip hop. Are the hackers of today laying the foundations for a new design?

----

14 WAYS TO GET HACKED

1. Design ingredients instead of complete products.
2. If you create a complete product, include an ingredients list.
3. Design for disassembly.
4. If the design was created digitally, ship the source files with the product. Better yet, just ship the source files. Don't flatten the layers.
5. Include version histories of your designs.
6. Design modules of larger systems.
7. Release your work half done.
8. Release your concepts as product. Let others make them.
9. Design products as platforms, and vice-versa.
10. Create a plugin library for others who want to add to your design.
11. Release a 'flat pack' option – it was all just pieces at some point.
12. Release beta versions.
13. If self-assembly is required, provide options for assembly. Create a wiki to allow your customers to do the same.
14. If it comes pre-assembled, include instructions for taking it apart.

About the Author

Scott Burnham, FRSA is a strategist and design researcher behind initiatives in over a dozen cities worldwide and more than thirty exhibitions in eight countries exploring new ideas for design and cities.

He is the creator and director of Reprogramming the City, a global initiative exploring the untapped potential of existing urban assets. He is the former director of The Netherlands Institute for Design's Trust Design project, and has addressed The World Bank, The World Urban Development Congress, and many other organizations on design strategies and urban futures. He is the author of Urban Play, Trust Design, and Reprogramming the City, as well as a contributor to publications ranging from The Guardian to Metropolis and Architizer.

In recognition of his work, Burnham was made a Fellow of the Royal Society for Arts, Manufacturers and Commerce in London in 2009. For more information see www.scottburnham.com

ENDNOTES

[i] Paul D Miller, aka DJ Spooky, Essay on and Interview with Manuel Delanda
http://djspooky.com/articles/essayonmanuel.html
[ii] Esquire Magazine, October 1971
[iii] See http://catb.org/~esr/faqs/hacker-howto.html
[iv] MAKE: Owner's Manual by "Mister Jalopy" See
http://makezine.com/04/ownyourown/
[v] Papanek, Victor (1971). *Design for the Real World: Human Ecology and Social Change*, New York, Pantheon Books . ISBN 0-394-47036-2.
[vi] Interview via Email, 28 July 2009
[vii] Discovery Channel Documentary, "The History of Hacking". Available online:
http://video.google.com/videoplay?docid=5464925144369700635#
[viii] Jan Chipchase, "Cultures of Repair, Innoation"
http://www.janchipchase.com/repaircultures
[ix] http://www.janchipchase.com/blog/archives/united-states/monterey/
[x] http://news.bbc.co.uk/1/hi/world/africa/8166196.stm
[xi] http://www.afrigadget.com/2009/08/15/a-pedal-powered-hacksaw-for-the-disabled/
[xii] See
http://www.recetasurbanas.net/index.php?idioma=ENG&ID=0002
[xiii] http://www.rebargroup.org/projects/parking/
[xiv] "Hacking's a snap in Legoland", CNET
http://news.cnet.com/Hackings-a-snap-in-Legoland/2100-1046_3-5865751.html
[xv] See http://www.hacklabs.org/en

www.ingramcontent.com/pod-product-compliance
Lightning Source LLC
Chambersburg PA
CBHW060531280326
41933CB00014B/3130